ATHENS GUIDE 2023

Discover The Rich History and Architecture of The City of the Violet Crown. With Recommended 2-4 Days Itinerary, Street and Satellite Maps for Easy Navigation

Williams Gill

Williams Gill

Copyright © 2023 by Williams Gill

All rights reserved.

No part of this book may be reproduced, stored in a retrieval system, or transmitted in any form or by any means, electronic, mechanical, photocopying, recording, scanning, or otherwise, without the prior written permission of the copyright owner.

DISCLAIMER

The author and publisher of this book have used their best efforts in preparing this book. The author and publisher make no representation or warranties with respect to the accuracy or completeness of the contents of this book and specifically disclaim any implied warranties of merchantability or fitness for a particular purpose. The author and publisher shall not be liable in any event for incidental or consequential damages in connection with, or arising out of, the furnishing, performance, or use of this book. Unless otherwise noted, all images and text are property of the author.

Williams Gill

Contents

INTRODUCTION 1
ABOUT ATHENS 5
PART I 9
BEFORE YOU GO 9
CHAPTER 1 11
   Preparing Your Trip to Athens 11
   When to go to Athens 13
   How to get to Athens 14
   Tips While travelling to Athens 15
   Visa and Entry Requirements 17
   Health and Safety Considerations 19
CHAPTER 2 21
   Overview of Athens 21
   Understanding Athens Culture and Etiquette 21
   Currency, Weather and Language 23
   Modern Arts and Architecture 27
   Navigating Athens: Transportation Options 31
Part II 35
Inside Athens 35

CHAPTER 3 37
Exploring Athens 37
Top 10 Attractions in Athens 39
Walking Tour of Athens 43
Eating and Drinking and Drinking in Athens 46
Shopping in Athens 49

CHAPTER 4 53
Day Trips from Athens 53
Delphi 54
Mycenae 55
Meteora 57
Nafplio 58
Epidaurus 60

CHAPTER 5 63
Museums and Cultural Attractions in Athens 63
Acropolis of Athens 64
National Archaeological Museum 66
Ancient Agora of Athens 67
Benaki Museum 69
Byzantine and Christian Museum 70
Hellenic Parliament 72

National Library of Greece 74

National Garden of Athens 75

CHAPTER 6 79

Safety and Security Tips for travelling in Athens .. 79

General safety Tips for travelling in Athens 80

Health and Medical Care in Athens 82

Common Health Concerns in Athens 86

Crimes to Watch Out for in Athens 88

CHAPTER 7 91

Accommodation in Athens 91

Hotels and Resorts 92

Camping 94

Parks and Resorts 98

CHAPTER 8 103

Eating and Dining in Athens 103

Athens Cuisine: A Culinary Adventure 103

Regional Athens Food to Try 108

Athens Wine 110

Best Places to Eat in Athens 113

Part III 117

Travel Essentials 117

CHAPTER 9	119
Financial Matters	119
Currency and Exchange Rates in Athens	119
Credit Card and ATMs in Athens	120
CHAPTER 10	123
Traveling With Kids or Pets	123
Pets	126
CHAPTER 11	129
Communication	129
Important Greek Words and Phrases	132
CONCLUSION	135
Notes	141
Notes	142
Notes	142

Williams Gill

INTRODUCTION

Welcome to the Athens Travel Guide! This book is the perfect companion for anyone considering a trip to the city of Athens, the capital and largest city in Greece. It is filled with invaluable information, tips, and advice to help you make the most of your journey. From the best places to eat and stay to the most beautiful sights to see, this guidebook will provide you with all the knowledge you need to have a memorable and enjoyable time in Athens.

Williams Gill

I'm Williams Gill, a travel writer and guidebook author. Since I was a kid, I have always been passionate about traveling. I have been to some of the most beautiful places in the world and I have seen some of the most amazing things. From the majestic landscapes of the Greek Isles to the historic monuments of Athens, I have experienced it all.

I have always been curious about Athens, so I decided to take a trip there. I was amazed at the beauty and history of the city. Everywhere I looked I could see ancient ruins, stunning monuments, and vibrant culture. I was sure I was in the right place.

I started my journey at the Acropolis of Athens. It was a breathtaking view, and I was in awe of the architecture and craftsmanship. After that, I visited the Parthenon, the Temple of Zeus, and the Ancient Agora of Athens. Everywhere I looked, I could see ancient ruins and monuments that had stood the test of time.

I also had the opportunity to explore the vibrant culture of Athens. I visited the bustling marketplaces, tasted the delicious local cuisine, and enjoyed the lively nightlife. Every day was a new adventure, and I was constantly learning about the history and culture of the city.

Athens is a city that is full of history, culture, and beauty. Everywhere I looked, I could see the past coming alive. I was inspired to write a travel guide that would give readers an inside look at the city. I wanted to share my experiences and the knowledge I had gained while exploring Athens.

My travel guide is packed with information about the best places to visit in Athens, the top restaurants and bars, the best shopping spots, and more. I also included tips and advice for travelers so they can make the most of their Athens experience.

I am confident that my travel guide will provide readers with an inside look at Athens and help them to get the most out of their visit. I encourage you to read my book and experience Athens in a way that you never could before.

Williams Gill

ABOUT ATHENS

Athens is the capital of Greece and one of the oldest cities in the world. It is located in the Attica region of Greece, on the southern tip of the Balkan Peninsula. It is the largest city in Greece and one of the most influential cities in the world.

The city has a rich history that dates back over 3,000 years. It is believed to have been founded around the year 1250 BC by King Theseus. In the 8th century BC, Athens became the most powerful city-state in the region, and in the 5th century BC, it was the leading city of ancient Greece.

It became the cultural center of the world, and its achievements in literature, philosophy, politics, and science have had a lasting impact on western civilization.

Athens was then conquered by the Romans in 146 BC and became part of the Roman Empire. It flourished during the Roman period and became the seat of the Roman governor. The city was sacked by Visigoths in AD 267 and by the Heruli in AD 395.

After the fall of the Roman Empire, Athens was ruled by the Byzantine Empire until it was captured by the Ottoman Turks in 1456. The city was ruled by the Ottoman Empire until 1821, when it declared independence. During the 19th century, Athens experienced a period of growth and modernization. It was made the capital of the newly formed Greek state in 1834.

Athens has been the capital of Greece since its independence. It is the country's economic, political, and cultural center. It is home to a number of important archaeological sites, including the Acropolis, the Parthenon, and the Temple of Zeus. The city is also home to a number of museums, galleries, and theaters, as well as a vibrant nightlife.

Athens is located in the region of Attica, at the southern tip of the Balkan Peninsula, near the Aegean Sea. It is surrounded by mountains, including Mount Lycabettus, Mount Hymettus, and Mount Pentelicus. The city's climate is mild and temperate, with hot summers and mild winters.

The people of Athens are known as Athenians. The city is home to a diverse population, with people from all over the world living in the city. The city is known for its vibrant culture, and it is a popular destination for tourists, who come to see the ancient monuments, explore the museums and galleries, and enjoy the lively nightlife.

Athens offers a unique blend of ancient and modern culture and is a must-see destination for anyone interested in exploring the history and culture of Greece.

Ancient Monument in Athens

Williams Gill

PART I

BEFORE YOU GO

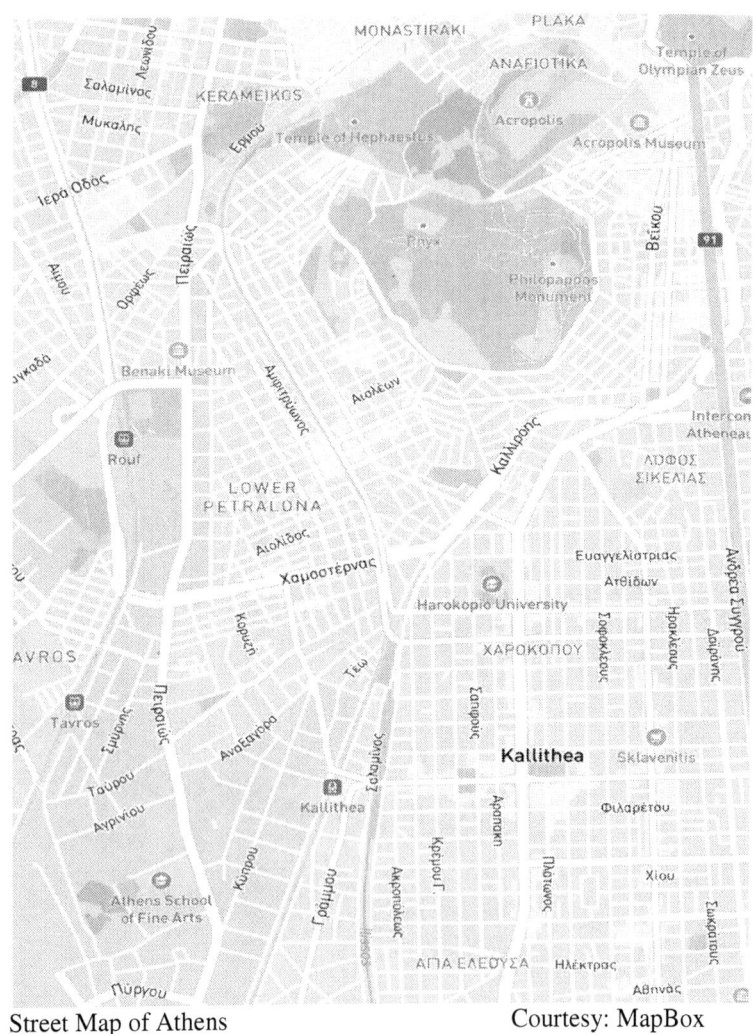

Street Map of Athens Courtesy: MapBox

CHAPTER 1

Preparing Your Trip to Athens

Planning a trip to Athens can seem intimidating, but with a few simple tips, it can be an enjoyable and stress-free experience. Begin by researching the city, its attractions, and the various neighborhoods and transportation options available. Booking accommodation is an important step, and there is a wide range of options to choose from, ranging from budget-friendly hostels to luxury hotels.

Once you have a better understanding of the city and have booked your accommodations, it's time to plan your itinerary. The Acropolis and Parthenon are the most popular attractions in the city, and should be on your list of things to see. Other must-visit attractions include the Temple of Zeus, the National Archaeological Museum, and the Ancient Agora.

When it comes to transportation, you can use public buses, trolleys, metro, or taxis to get around. It's important to note that the public transportation system in Athens can be confusing, so take the time to familiarize yourself with it before you go.

Finally, make sure to take time to explore the city's vibrant nightlife and gastronomy scene. Athens has plenty of bustling bars, clubs, and restaurants, so you won't have a problem finding something to do.

By following these tips, you'll be well on your way to a memorable and stress-free trip to Athens. Have a great time!

When to go to Athens

Athens is a great destination all year round, though the best times to visit are from March to May and from September to October. During these months, the temperatures are mild and the crowds are fewer than in the peak seasons of summer and winter.

Athens has a Mediterranean climate, with hot and dry summers and mild winters. The temperature can reach up to 40 Celsius (104 Fahrenheit) in the summer months, so it is best to avoid this period if you don't like the heat.

In the spring, temperatures are mild, with an average of around 17 Celsius (62 Fahrenheit). This is the best time for sightseeing, as the days are warm and sunny, and there is less humidity than in the summer.

In the autumn, the weather is still pleasant and the temperatures remain mild, with an average of around 17 Celsius (62 Fahrenheit). This is the perfect time to visit Athens, as the crowds are smaller and the prices are lower.

No matter what time of the year you choose to visit, Athens is sure to offer a memorable experience. With its ancient ruins, vibrant culture, and stunning views, it is a city that is sure to delight.

How to get to Athens

Athens, the birthplace of democracy and one of the oldest cities in the world, is easily accessible from many destinations.

The most popular way to get to Athens is by air. Athens International Airport is the primary airport serving the city and is located just 17 miles from the city center. Major airlines such as British Airways, KLM, Lufthansa, and Aegean Airlines offer direct flights to Athens from many international cities.

Athens is also easily accessible by train. There are daily connections from many European cities, including Paris, Rome, and Istanbul. The main train station in Athens is the Larissa Station, located just a few blocks from the Acropolis.

For those traveling by car, Athens can be reached via several highways. The A1 connects Athens to Thessaloniki in the north, while the A6 connects Athens to Patras in the west.

Finally, Athens can be reached by ferry. The city's main port is the Port of Piraeus, located just outside of Athens. Ferries from the port connect Athens to many of the Greek islands, as well as other European cities such as Venice and Bari.

Tips While travelling to Athens

1. **Do your research:** Before you travel to Athens, make sure to do your research about the city, its attractions, culture, and customs. This will help you

make the most of your trip and ensure you have a great experience.

2. **Pack light:** Athens is a city that's easy to explore on foot, so you won't need to bring a lot of luggage. Pack light and bring only essential items, since you'll likely be doing a lot of walking.

3. **Try the local cuisine:** Greek cuisine is world-renowned for its delicious flavors, so make sure you take the time to sample some of the local dishes.

From gyros to moussaka, you're sure to find something you like.

4. **Visit the Acropolis:** The Acropolis is one of the most famous landmarks in Athens, and a must-see for anyone visiting the city. Take some time to explore the ancient ruins and get a glimpse into the city's history.

5. **Shop in Plaka:** Plaka is Athens' oldest neighborhood and one of the most charming places to shop. Whether you're looking for souvenirs or local

crafts and jewelry, you're sure to find something special.

6. **Take a day trip:** Athens is surrounded by many famous sights and attractions, so don't miss the chance to take a day trip to places like Delphi or Cape Sounion.

7. **Use public transport:** Athens has an efficient public transport system that's easy to use. It's a great way to get around the city and save money at the same time.

8. **Stay safe:** When travelling to Athens, make sure to stay alert and aware of your surroundings. Carry a copy of your passport in case of an emergency, and avoid travelling alone at night.

Visa and Entry Requirements

Visitors to Athens must have a valid passport to enter the country. Depending on the length of the stay, travelers may be required to obtain a visa in advance.

Citizens of EU countries do not need a visa to enter Greece, while citizens of other countries may need to apply for a Schengen visa. This visa is valid for up to 90 days and can be used to travel to other countries in the Schengen area.

1. **Valid Passport:** All travelers must present a valid passport that is valid for at least six months beyond the date of entry.

2. **Tourist Visa:** Depending on nationality, travelers may need to obtain a tourist visa for entry to Athens. This can be done through the Greek embassy or consulate in your home country.

3. **Proof of Financial Support:** Travelers may need to show proof of financial support for the duration of their trip. This can be in the form of a bank statement showing sufficient funds or a credit card statement.

4. **Round-Trip Ticket:** Travelers must present a round-trip ticket, either physical or electronic, showing their departure date from Athens.

5. **Health Insurance:** Travelers may need to present proof of health insurance valid for the duration of their stay in Athens.

In addition, visitors must also have proof of sufficient funds for the duration of their stay in Greece. They may also need to show proof of travel insurance in case of an emergency. Finally, travelers should check the entry requirements for their final destination to ensure they are able to enter the country.

Health and Safety Considerations

1. **Vaccinations:** Before travelling to Athens, make sure you are up to date with all necessary vaccinations. This includes getting boosters for any vaccines you already have, as well as getting any new vaccines that may be recommended for the region. Speak to your doctor about what vaccinations are needed for your trip.

2. **Sun Safety:** Athens can get very hot and sunny throughout the year. Be sure to protect yourself from

the sun by wearing sunscreen, hats and sunglasses, and drinking plenty of water.

3. **Food Safety:** Be aware of what you eat and where you buy it from. Avoid eating street food and opt for restaurants with good reviews. Make sure food is cooked properly and served at the right temperature.

4. **Water Safety:** Tap water in Athens is generally safe to drink. However, it is recommended to drink bottled or filtered water to avoid any potential risks.

5. **Crime:** Athens is generally a safe city, but it is still important to be aware of your surroundings and take the necessary precautions to stay safe. Avoid carrying large amounts of cash and keep your belongings close to you.

6. **Medical Care:** Make sure you have the right travel insurance before you go to Athens. Have the contact details of your insurance provider and a list of local medical facilities in case of any medical emergencies.

CHAPTER 2

Overview of Athens

Understanding Athens Culture and Etiquette

Athens is a city steeped in history and culture. From the iconic Acropolis to the vibrant nightlife, Athens has something for everyone. But when it comes to etiquette, Athens has its own unique set of customs and traditions that visitors should be aware of before visiting.

The Greek language is the official language of Athens and is spoken by most of the city's inhabitants. While English is also widely spoken, it's always polite and appreciated to learn a few basic phrases in Greek.

In Athens, it is considered polite to greet people with a kiss on both cheeks, regardless of their gender. It is also customary to remove your shoes when entering someone's home.

When dining in Athens, it is important to observe the proper etiquette. Table manners are expected to be followed, with utensils being used in the correct order and food being eaten with the right hand. It is also important to remember that it is considered rude to leave food on your plate.

When it comes to clothing, Athens is a conservative city and visitors should dress appropriately. For men, long trousers and a shirt are usually acceptable, while women should avoid revealing clothing.

Athens is home to a vibrant nightlife and visitors should be aware that the city has its own unique drinking culture. It is important to remember that public drunkenness is frowned upon and visitors should always drink responsibly.

Finally, it is important to remember that Athens is a city with deep religious roots. As such, visitors should be aware of the religious customs and traditions in the city and always be respectful of them.

By following these guidelines, visitors to Athens can ensure that they enjoy their stay without offending anyone or causing any cultural faux pas.

Currency, Weather and Language

Athens, the capital of Greece, is a vibrant and beautiful city full of culture, history, and heritage. A trip to Athens is a must for anyone looking to explore the rich history of the city, as well as to experience the unique and charming culture.

When planning your trip to Athens, it's important to understand the local currency and language, as they are essential for navigating and enjoying the city.

Currency

The official currency of Greece is the euro, abbreviated as EUR. The euro is the currency for the European Union, and it is accepted throughout the country. Currency exchange is available at airports, banks, and certain post offices.

It's important to note that some establishments may not accept euros, so it's always best to have some local currency on hand. ATMs are also a great way to obtain cash, but make sure to check with your bank beforehand to ensure you won't incur any extra fees. Credit and debit cards are accepted at most places, but it's always recommended to carry cash for smaller purchases.

Language

The official language of Greece is Greek, but English is widely spoken in Athens. You'll find that most locals understand and can speak English, so there should be no language barrier when it comes to navigating the city. However, it's always polite to learn some basic phrases in the local language, as it's a great way to interact with locals and make the most of your trip. In this guide you would learn some basic Greek language.

With a little bit of preparation, you'll be able to make the most of your trip to Athens. Understanding the local currency and language will help you navigate the city and ensure you have a wonderful trip.

Weather

Athens is a Mediterranean city, and the weather is typical of the region. Summers are hot and dry, with temperatures often reaching into the mid-30s Celsius (mid-90s Fahrenheit).

Winters, on the other hand, are mild and wet, with temperatures rarely dropping below zero Celsius (32 Fahrenheit).

Rainfall is common throughout the year, with the most precipitation occurring in the winter months. It's a good idea to bring a light jacket, as temperatures can drop quickly in the evenings. It's also important to wear sunscreen, as the sun can be very powerful in the summer months.

Modern Arts and Architecture

Athens, the capital of Greece, is an ancient city with a rich history of art and architecture that has been preserved and appreciated for centuries. From the ancient Acropolis to the more contemporary works of modern Athens, this city offers a wide variety of architectural styles and art forms for visitors to explore and appreciate.

The Acropolis is the most iconic landmark of Athens and an absolute must-see for anyone visiting the city. This ancient citadel was built between 447-438 BC and is home to many of the oldest and most impressive monuments of Ancient Greece, including the Parthenon, the Temple of Athena Nike and the Erectheum. The Acropolis is a testament to the glory of Ancient Greece, and is a must-visit attraction when in Athens.

Another impressive piece of architecture in Athens is the **Temple of Olympian Zeus**. Located near the Acropolis, this temple was built in the 6th century BC and is the largest temple in Ancient Greece.

The temple is made up of 104 Corinthian columns and is one of the most impressive examples of ancient Greek architecture.

The Syntagma Square is another important landmark in Athens. This square is the political center of the city and is home to the Greek Parliament building. This building is a grand example of neoclassical architecture, with its impressive facade and impressive colonnades. The Tomb of the Unknown Soldier is also located in the square, and is a moving reminder of the sacrifices made by the people of Greece during wartime.

In addition to its ancient monuments, Athens is also home to many impressive examples of modern art and architecture. The National Museum of Contemporary Art is a great place to start when exploring the city's art scene. Located in the former Athens Brewery, this museum houses a wide range of modern artworks from artists all over the world.

The Stavros Niarchos Foundation Cultural Center is another impressive piece of modern architecture in Athens. This center was designed by the renowned Italian architect Renzo Piano and opened in 2016. It is home to the National Library of Greece, the Greek National Opera and the National Observatory of Athens.

Athens is also home to a number of impressive examples of street art. The **Psiri** neighborhood is a great place to explore street art, as it is home to some of the most impressive works of graffiti, murals and stencils in the city.

Athens is a city with a rich history of art and architecture. Whether you are looking for ancient monuments, impressive examples of neoclassical architecture, or the vibrant street art of the city, Athens is sure to provide something to satisfy all tastes.

Navigating Athens: Transportation Options

Athens is a bustling metropolis and a great travel destination for those looking to explore the beauty and culture of Greece. While the city has many attractions, the transportation system is one of the most important things to consider when planning your trip. Fortunately, getting around in Athens is relatively easy, with several options available to visitors.

The most popular way of getting around Athens is via the metro system. This modern, efficient and clean system is made up of three lines, connecting the main areas of the city. The ticket price is fairly reasonable and the metro runs from around 5.30am until midnight, with some lines running late-night services on weekends. There are also regular buses running throughout the city and to the nearby suburbs, with tickets being sold at the metro stations, kiosks and aboard the buses.

Taxis are also a convenient option, with many available around the city and easy to flag down. It's important to make sure you agree on the fare with the driver before getting in, as some may try to take advantage of a tourist. Alternatively, you can use one of the many ride-sharing apps available in Athens, such as Uber, Beat or Taxibeat.

For those looking to explore Athens at their own pace, there are several car rental companies offering a range of vehicles.

The cost depends on the size of the car and the length of the rental, so it's important to shop around for the best deal. It's also important to note that driving in Athens can be quite chaotic, with traffic jams being a common occurrence.

Cycling is also a great way to get around Athens, with dedicated bike lanes in many areas of the city. There are several companies offering bike rentals, with daily, weekly and monthly rates available. Most of them also offer guided bike tours to explore the city, which can be a great way to get to know the city.

Finally, Athens also has a ferry system that connects the city to the nearby islands of Aegina, Poros and Hydra. Ferries run daily between the islands and the main port of Piraeus, with tickets varying depending on the route and the time of year.

Overall, there are several options available for getting around Athens, making it easy to explore the city and its surroundings.

Whether you're using the metro, a taxi, a bike or a ferry, you'll find the transport system in Athens to be efficient and affordable.

Boat and Ferry Park, Athens

Williams Gill

Part II

Inside Athens

Busy Street of Athens

CHAPTER 3

Exploring Athens

E xploring Athens is an exciting and unforgettable experience. This historic city is full of ancient ruins, stunning architecture, and vibrant culture. Visitors can explore the Acropolis, the ancient city walls, the Parthenon, the Temple of Zeus, the Theatre of Dionysus, and the Ancient Agora. The Acropolis Museum is one of the top attractions in the city and offers an immersive look into the past.

There are also a variety of public parks, museums, galleries, and archaeological sites to explore. Athens also has an active nightlife, with a wide selection of bars, clubs, and restaurants. In addition, the city offers a range of shopping opportunities, from traditional markets to modern boutiques. No matter what your interests are, Athens has something for everyone.

Night view of the beautiful city

Top 10 Attractions in Athens

1. **Acropolis of Athens** – The Acropolis of Athens is a UNESCO World Heritage Site and one of the most recognizable landmarks in the world. It is an ancient citadel located on a rocky outcrop above the city of Athens.

This iconic site is home to several ancient structures, including the Parthenon and the Erectheion. It is a must-see for anyone visiting Athens, and offers stunning views of the city.

2. **The Temple of Olympian Zeus** – This ancient temple is the largest temple of classical antiquity and is located in the center of Athens. It was built in the 6th century BC and was dedicated to the king of gods, Zeus. Today, only 15 of its 104 original columns remain standing.

3. **The Acropolis Museum** – The Acropolis Museum is dedicated to the history and artifacts of Ancient Greece, and is located at the base of the Acropolis.

It features a large collection of sculptures and artifacts from the Parthenon, as well as other ancient monuments.

4. **The National Archaeological Museum** – The National Archaeological Museum is the largest museum in Greece, and is home to an impressive collection of Greek antiquities. It is located in the city center and is a must-see for anyone interested in Greek history.

5. **Ancient Agora of Athens** – The Ancient Agora of Athens was a public gathering place in ancient Greece, and is home to the ruins of several ancient monuments, including the Temple of Hephaestus. It is located in the heart of the city and is a great place to explore the history of Athens.

6. **Plaka** – Plaka is the oldest neighborhood in Athens, and is characterized by its winding cobblestone streets and beautiful neoclassical buildings.

It is a great place to explore traditional Greek restaurants and shops, as well as some of the city's most iconic monuments.

7. **Monastiraki** – Monastiraki is a bustling neighborhood located in the center of Athens. It is home to the city's famous flea market, as well as plenty of traditional Greek restaurants and cafes.

8. **The National Garden of Athens** – The National Garden of Athens is a lush green oasis located in the heart of the city.

It is a great place to relax and escape the hustle and bustle of the city, as well as explore its many pathways, ponds, and statues.

9. **Lycabettus Hill** – Lycabettus Hill is the highest point in Athens and offers stunning views of the city. It is home to a funicular railway, as well as a theatre, restaurant, and cafe.

10. **Mount Lycabettus** – Mount Lycabettus is the second highest point in Athens and is home to the Chapel of Agios Georgios. It is a popular spot for hikes and offers beautiful views of the city.

Walking Tour of Athens

Athens is a city steeped in history, and a walking tour of the city is the perfect way to explore its many layers of culture and heritage. From the ancient ruins of the Acropolis and the Parthenon, to the winding streets of the Plaka, the city offers a wealth of sights to discover.

For a comprehensive walking tour of Athens, begin at the Acropolis, the most iconic symbol of the city. Here, you can visit the Parthenon, the Temple of Athena Nike, the Erechtheion, and the Propylaea.

Along the way, you can admire the spectacular views of the city and learn about the incredible history of this ancient site.

Next, walk to the Plaka, a bustling neighbourhood in the heart of Athens. Here, you can explore the narrow cobbled streets and admire the traditional Greek architecture. Wander through the winding alleys and discover hidden gems such as the Benaki Museum, the Ancient Agora, and the picturesque Anafiotika district.

Your next stop should be the Panathenaic Stadium, the site of the first modern Olympic Games in 1896. Here, you can learn about the history of the Games and appreciate the impressive engineering feat that is the stadium.

Afterwards, stroll through the National Gardens, a lush green haven in the centre of Athens. Here, you can admire the beautiful foliage and fountains, and take a break from the hustle and bustle of the city.

Continue your walking tour at the Museum of the City of Athens, which provides a detailed overview of the city's past, present and future.

Then, take a stroll through Syntagma Square, the main square of Athens and the site of the Parliament building.

Finally, end your tour at the Monastiraki Flea Market, a vibrant shopping district full of small stalls selling everything from souvenirs to vintage clothes. Here, you can pick up a few souvenirs to take home.

Athens is a city full of history and culture, and a walking tour is the perfect way to explore its many layers. With a comprehensive tour of the city, you can visit some of the most iconic sites and enjoy the vibrant atmosphere of the city.

Eating and Drinking and Drinking in Athens

Exploring the culinary delights of Athens is a must for any traveler. As the capital of Greece, the city is home to a wide variety of restaurants, bars, and eateries, all offering a unique taste of Athens.

When it comes to drinks, Athens has a deep-rooted coffee culture. Whether it's a traditional Greek coffee or a modern espresso, you'll find numerous cafes and coffee shops to choose from. The city also boasts a wide selection of tea, wine, and beer.

When it comes to food, Athens offers a vast selection of dishes. For a classic Greek experience, try the famous moussaka. This hearty dish, made of layered eggplant, ground meat, and a creamy béchamel sauce is the perfect comfort food. Souvlaki, a popular Greek street food, is another must-try. This dish consists of grilled meat, usually pork or chicken, served on a skewer and paired with tzatziki, a creamy yogurt-based sauce.

Greek cuisine is known for its freshness and flavor, so don't miss out on Athens' many traditional eateries. One of the most popular spots is the Psistaria, a tavern-style restaurant where you can enjoy grilled meats and vegetables.

Another great option is the Taverna, a more upscale restaurant that serves a variety of Greek dishes.

For a more modern take on Greek cuisine, try one of Athens' many contemporary restaurants. These restaurants often feature a mix of traditional Greek dishes with a modern twist. For example, you can find dishes like Moussaka Pizza, which is a combination of the classic moussaka and a thin-crust pizza.

And for those looking for a more international experience, Athens has plenty of options. From Chinese to Indian, you'll find a wide selection of restaurants serving up all kinds of global cuisines.

No matter what kind of food you're in the mood for, Athens has something to offer. Whether it's a classic Greek dish or something more exotic, the city's culinary scene is sure to impress. So make sure to take some time to explore Athens' many eateries and sample the city's unique flavors.

Shopping in Athens

Shopping in Athens is one of the most exciting experiences in the city. Athens is known for its vibrant street markets, bustling shopping districts, and chic boutiques.

Whether you are looking for souvenirs to take home, traditional Greek goods, or designer brands, you will find it all in Athens.

The Plaka area is one of the most popular shopping destinations in Athens. The Plaka is a historic and picturesque neighborhood located at the foot of the Acropolis. It is filled with cobbled streets lined with traditional shops and restaurants. Here you can find all kinds of souvenirs, from handcrafted jewelry to local pottery and olive wood carvings. You can also find traditional clothing and other Greek goods.

The Monastiraki district is another great place for shopping in Athens. This area is located near the Acropolis and is known for its flea and antique markets. On Sundays, the streets of Monastiraki are filled with vendors selling everything from vintage clothing to antiques.

The Ermou Street area is one of the most popular shopping streets in Athens. This pedestrianized street is filled with stores selling everything from clothing to souvenirs. The vast selection of shops makes Ermou Street a great place to find the perfect gift or souvenir.

The Kolonaki district is the chic shopping area of Athens. This is where you will find the most upscale boutiques and designer stores. It is also home to the famous Benaki Museum, which displays a collection of Greek artifacts.

The Central Market is one of the most famous markets in Athens. Located in the center of the city, this market is known for its fresh produce, spices, and local delicacies. It is a great place to find traditional Greek ingredients and souvenirs.

If you are looking for a great shopping experience in Athens, then make sure to check out these places. From traditional Greek goods to designer brands, there is something for everyone in Athens.

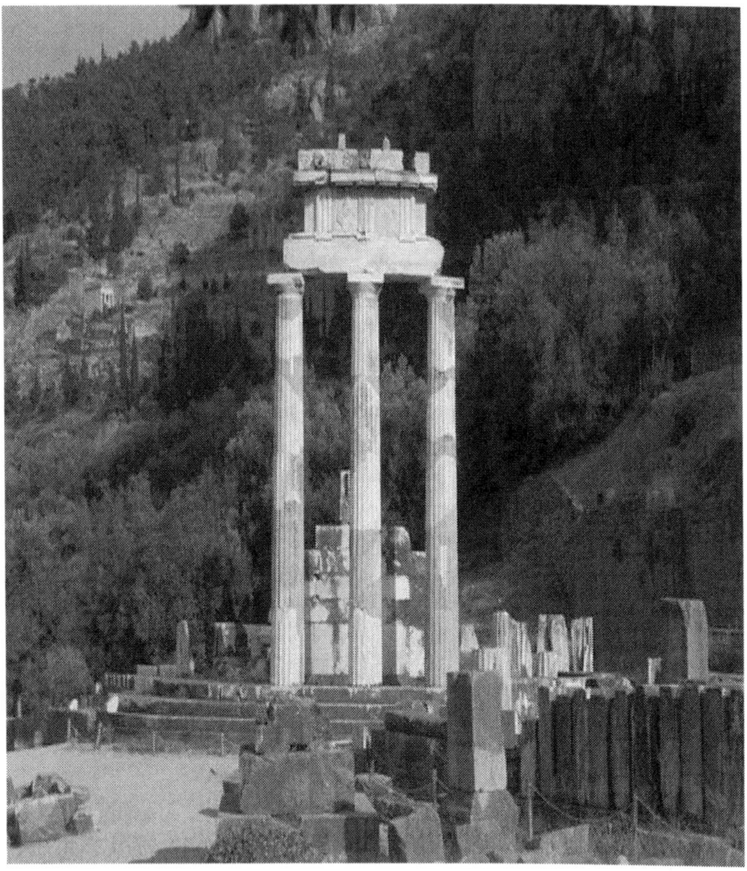

CHAPTER 4

Day Trips from Athens

Athens is a great city to explore, but there are many exciting day trips from Athens that offer travelers a chance to experience the beauty of the region. From stunning beaches and ancient sites to dramatic mountain ranges and charming villages, the day trips around Athens are an ideal way to get the most out of your stay.

Delphi

Located approximately three hours away from Athens, Delphi is an ancient Greek city steeped in history and culture. The city contains many ancient archaeological sites, including the Temple of Apollo, the Temple of Athena, the Ancient Theatre, and the Sanctuary of Athena.

Delphi is an archaeological site in Greece located on the slopes of Mount Parnassus in central Greece. It is also known as the **'navel of the world'**, because according to Ancient Greek mythology, Zeus released two eagles from the ends of the universe, and they met in Delphi. It was an important religious centre in ancient Greece, and the site of the Oracle of Delphi.

The sanctuary of Apollo was the most important religious site in ancient Greece, and it was here that the oracle of Delphi was located. The Oracle of Delphi was a powerful and influential religious figure in the ancient Greek world. Visitors would come from all over the Greek world to consult the oracle on matters of politics, war, and other important decisions.

The ruins of Delphi are an important archaeological site, and include the Temple of Apollo, the Theatre of Delphi, and the Delphi Museum. The archaeological site is listed as a UNESCO World Heritage Site, and it is one of the most popular tourist attractions in Greece.

Mycenae

Mycenae is an ancient city located approximately two hours away from Athens. The city was once the seat of power for the Mycenaean civilization and is home to the famous Lion Gate, the Grave Circle A, the Treasury of Atreus, and the Palace of Agamemnon. Mycenae is an ancient city located in the Peloponnese region of Greece. It was one of the most important cities of the Mycenaean civilization, and it was the political, economic and religious center of the area.

It was founded in the 16th century BC and was a powerful city-state until it was destroyed by the Dorians in the early 11th century BC.

Mycenae is home to some of the most important archaeological sites in Greece, including the ruins of the citadel, which served as the royal palace of the Mycenaean kings. Inside the ruins, visitors can explore the famous Lion Gate, the Grave Circle A and the Treasury of Atreus. The site also features several other monuments, such as the temple of Apollo, the palace complex and the ancient theatre.

Mycenae is located in the northeastern part of the Peloponnese, about 90 km (56 miles) southwest of Athens. It lies near the modern-day village of Mykines, in the Argolis prefecture. It is accessible by car, bus or train and is a popular tourist destination.

Meteora

Meteora is a complex of monasteries located about three hours away from Athens.

The monasteries are perched atop towering sandstone rocks and offer breathtaking views of the surrounding landscape. Meteora is a spectacular region of Greece known for its incredible rock formations and monasteries located on top of the towering rocks. The area is located in the Thessaly region of central Greece, close to the city of Kalambaka.

Meteora is an extraordinary geological phenomenon, with huge sandstone and conglomerate rock formations that soar up to 400 meters above sea level. The stunning landscape is home to a total of 24 monasteries, six of which are still in operation today.

The monasteries of Meteora are a UNESCO World Heritage Site, as they are some of the oldest and most historically significant monasteries in Greece.

The monasteries were founded by monks in the 14th century, and many of them remain in active use today.

Meteora is a popular tourist destination, attracting visitors from all over the world who come to take in the stunning views and explore the monasteries. The area also offers a variety of hiking, climbing and other outdoor activities.

Nafplio

Nafplio is a beautiful seaside town located about two hours away from Athens. The town is known for its romantic atmosphere and is a popular destination for tourists seeking a relaxing day trip. Nafplio is a picturesque port city located on the Peloponnese peninsula in the eastern part of the Peloponnese region in Greece. It is a popular tourist destination due to its historic sites, charming narrow streets, and stunning views of the sea.

Nafplio was the first capital of Greece during the early 19th century and is home to some of the most important monuments of Greece. The city is situated on the Argolic Gulf, on the north coast of the Peloponnese, about 75 kilometers (47 miles) southeast of Athens. The old town of Nafplio is a maze of narrow streets lined with beautiful neoclassical mansions, Byzantine churches, and Venetian fortresses. The city is also home to many archaeological sites, including the ancient theater of Epidaurus.

There are numerous beaches in the area, including Kondylaki Beach and Karathonas Beach. Other attractions include the archaeological museum, the Bourtzi Fortress, the Palamidi Fortress, and the Archaeological Museum of Nafplio.

Epidaurus

Epidaurus is an ancient city located about two hours away from Athens. The city is home to the famous Epidaurus Theatre, which is one of the best preserved theatres from the classical period. The theatre is also known for its excellent acoustics and is still used for theatrical performances today.

Epidaurus is an ancient city located in the northeastern Peloponnese region of Greece. It is situated in the Argolid plain, some 50km southwest of Corinth and 65km from Athens. It is renowned for its ancient theatre and sanctuary of Asklepios, the god of healing.

The theatre at Epidaurus is a remarkable structure, seating up to 14,000 people and is renowned for its excellent acoustics.

It was constructed in the 4th century BC and is still used today for performances of ancient Greek tragedies.

The Sanctuary of Asklepios is a complex of buildings dedicated to the healing god. It was first established in the 4th century BC and was built around a sacred spring. The sanctuary included a hospital, temple, gymnasium and theatre.

Epidaurus is also home to the Archaeological Museum, which houses a vast collection of artifacts and sculptures from the ancient city.

Epidaurus is located close to the sea and is surrounded by a beautiful landscape, with a backdrop of mountains and lush vegetation. It is a popular destination for tourists, who come to explore its ancient ruins and enjoy the tranquility of its natural environment.

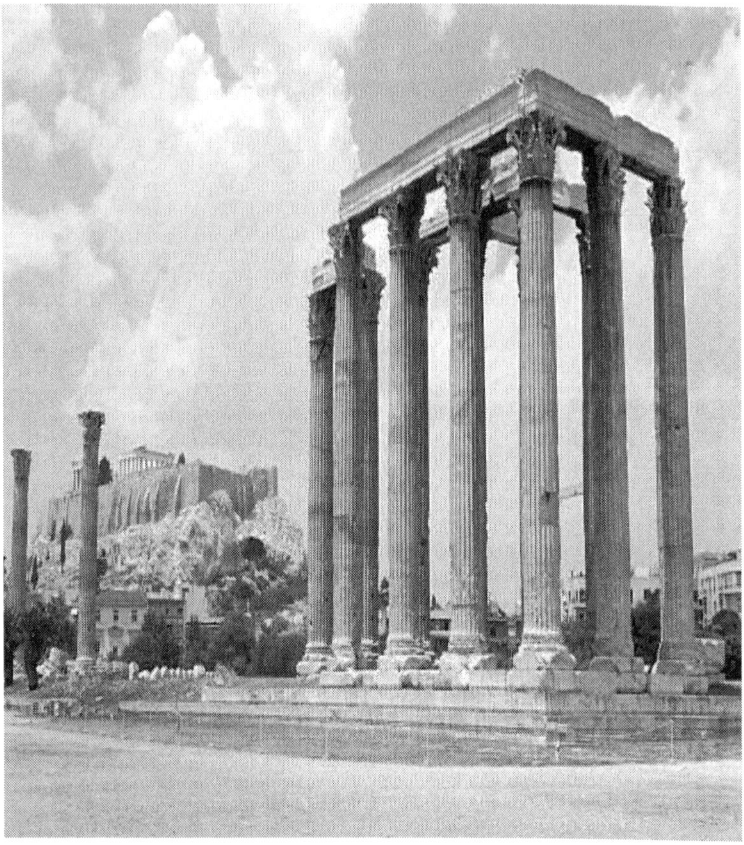

Williams Gill

CHAPTER 5

Museums and Cultural Attractions in Athens

Athens is a vibrant city full of awe-inspiring historical sites, museums, and attractions. The Acropolis of Athens, a UNESCO World Heritage site, is one of the most famous landmarks in the world. Here, you can explore the remains of the ancient Greek city, including the Parthenon, the Propylaea, the Erechtheion, and the Temple of Athena Nike.

Other cultural attractions include the National Archaeological Museum, the Benaki Museum, the Byzantine and Christian Museum, and the Cycladic Art Museum. Additionally, the National Garden, Lycabettus Hill, and Plaka-Monastiraki are popular outdoor attractions with stunning views of the city.

Acropolis of Athens

The Acropolis Museum is an archaeological museum focused on the findings of the archaeological site of the Acropolis of Athens. The museum was built to house every artifact found on the rock and on its feet, from the Greek Bronze Age to Roman and Byzantine Greece. It is located by the southeastern slope of the Acropolis hill, in the area of Makrygianni.

The museum was built between 1975 and 2009 and its design was conducted by the Swiss-German architect Bernard Tschumi.

It was opened to the public in 2009 and houses more than 4,000 artifacts. The museum has a total area of 14,000 square meters and its main entrance is situated on Dionysiou Areopagitou Street, right next to the hill of the Acropolis.

The museum is a three-story building that stands out for its modern design which is a contrast to the classical ruins it exhibits.

It has 18 galleries and the artifacts are presented in chronological order, from the Neolithic period to the end of the Roman era.

The museum also has a series of study rooms, a library, a lab for restoration and a separate café and restaurant. It offers various educational programs and activities for children and adults. It also has a large garden and an open courtyard where visitors can take a break and enjoy the stunning views of the Acropolis.

The Acropolis Museum is a major attraction in Athens and it is visited by thousands of tourists every year.

It is a must-visit for anyone who is interested in the history and culture of Greece.

National Archaeological Museum

The National Archaeological Museum of Athens is the largest archaeological museum in Greece and one of the most important museums in the world devoted to ancient Greek art. Located in the centre of Athens, the museum houses some of the most important artifacts from the Greek Bronze Age, as well as other important ancient Greek artifacts. The museum first opened its doors in 1829 and was initially housed in the room of the University of Athens. In 1889, it moved to its current location in a building designed by architect Panos Kalkos.

The museum houses artifacts from all over the Greek world, including sculptures, pottery, jewelry, coins, and artifacts from the Minoan, Cycladic, Mycenaean and Classical periods.

The museum also features a large number of objects from the Roman period, including mosaics, coins, and sculptures. The museum's collection includes a number of significant archaeological finds such as the Antikythera Mechanism, which is an ancient device used to track the movement of celestial bodies, and the Mask of Agamemnon.

The National Archaeological Museum is located on Patission Street in Athens, near the intersection of Amalias Avenue and Vasilissis Sofias Avenue. It is easily accessible from the city center on the Red Line of the Athens Metro. The museum is open daily from 8 am to 8 pm and is closed on Mondays. Visitors can purchase tickets in the museum's lobby or online.

Ancient Agora of Athens

The Ancient Agora of Athens is an archaeological site located in the heart of the city, in the area of Monastiraki.

It was the center of public life in ancient Athens, as it was the site of the marketplace, the public assembly, and the political and judicial courts.

In ancient times, the Agora was a bustling marketplace for goods and services, and it was the social center of the city. It was home to the ancient temple of Hephaestus and the Stoa of Attalos, as well as a variety of other public buildings.

The Agora was also the site of the world's first democracy, as it was here that the citizens of Athens were able to meet and discuss the laws and policies of the city. It was also the site of the trial of Socrates in 399 BC.

Today, the Agora is filled with ruins of ancient structures and artifacts, and it is one of the most important archaeological sites in the world. It has been designated a UNESCO World Heritage Site and is a popular spot for visitors to explore the history of the city. The site is open daily to visitors, and guided tours are available.

Benaki Museum

The Benaki Museum is a historical museum located in the Greek capital of Athens. Founded in 1930, it is one of the largest museums in Greece and home to more than 20,000 objects from across the country, from antiquity to the present day.

The museum is located in the historic centre of Athens, in the Koukaki district. It occupies two large neoclassical buildings, the old building, which was built in 1842 and was once home to the Benaki family, and the new building, which was opened in 2000 and houses the museum's archaeological collections.

The museum's collections span a wide range of disciplines, from archaeology to modern art, and include paintings, sculptures, pottery, jewellery, coins, weapons, furniture, textiles, and manuscripts.

The museum also has a library and research centre, as well as a children's museum and a cafe.

The Benaki Museum is open to the public and admission is free of charge. It is a popular tourist attraction and offers a wide range of educational and cultural activities, such as lectures, seminars, film screenings, and guided tours. It also hosts a variety of temporary exhibitions throughout the year, focusing on topics such as ancient Greek art, Byzantine art, and Islamic art.

The Benaki Museum is one of Athens' most important cultural institutions and a must-visit destination for anyone interested in the history and culture of Greece.

Byzantine and Christian Museum

The Byzantine and Christian Museum in Athens is one of the most popular tourist attractions in the city. Located in the heart of the Plaka district, the museum houses a stunning collection of Byzantine and Christian artifacts from the 4th to the 19th century.

The museum was originally founded in 1914 by the Greek archaeologist, Ioannis Touratsoglou, and was later expanded and renovated in the 1950s.

The museum is divided into three main sections, each focusing on a different era of Christian and Byzantine history. The first section is devoted to the early Christian period, featuring artifacts from the 4th to the 7th centuries. This section includes several icons from the 6th century, as well as a collection of liturgical vessels, fragments of frescoes, and mosaics.

The second section of the museum is dedicated to the Byzantine period, including artifacts from the 8th to the 15th centuries. This section showcases sculptures, frescoes, manuscripts, and panels of icons from the Byzantine period.

The third section of the museum focuses on the post-Byzantine period, from the 16th to the 19th centuries. This section includes a variety of artifacts from the

Ottoman period, including coins, jewelry, and manuscripts.

Hellenic Parliament

The Hellenic Parliament (Vouli) is the supreme decision-making body of the Hellenic Republic and is located in Syntagma Square in the centre of Athens. It is a unicameral legislature with 300 members, elected for a four-year term by a system of reinforced proportional representation in 56 multi-seat constituencies. The Parliament is housed within the Old Royal Palace, a 19th-century Neoclassical building which was the original home of the Greek monarchy.

The Hellenic Parliament is the most important political institution in Greece, as it is the legislative branch of government. It is the highest decision-making body in the Greek political system and is responsible for enacting laws, ratifying international agreements, approving the national budget and overseeing the activities of the executive branch. It is also responsible for electing the President of the Republic and the Prime Minister.

The Parliament is a symbol of democracy and is an important tourist attraction in Athens, drawing many visitors to the square in front of the building. The square is also the site of the Changing of the Guard, a popular ceremony involving the Presidential Guard, which takes place daily at noon.

The Parliament building itself is an impressive and imposing structure, with a long history and many stories to tell. It was built in the mid-19th century as the home of the Greek Royal family and has undergone several renovations over the years.

It has a large central edifice and two wings, surrounded by gardens and statues. The interior is decorated with a mix of marble and wood, with the grand staircase and the hall of the Senate being particularly impressive.

The Hellenic Parliament is a key landmark in the city of Athens and a symbol of Greek democracy. It has a long and fascinating history and is a must-see for visitors to the city.

National Library of Greece

The National Library of Greece is located in the city of Athens and is the largest library in Greece and the most important research library in the country. It is situated on Panepistimiou Street in the center of the city and is part of the Academy of Athens complex.

The building was designed by the Danish architect Theophil Hansen and was completed in 1887. It is one of the most important Neoclassical buildings in Athens and is considered to be one of the finest examples of Neoclassical architecture in the world.

The library currently houses over 4.5 million volumes and is one of the largest collections in the world.

It includes works from the 16th century to the present day and its collections cover a wide range of topics, from literature and philosophy to religion and science.

The library is open to the public and offers a variety of services, including exhibitions, lectures, seminars, and other educational activities. It also houses a variety of special collections, such as rare books, manuscripts, maps, and photographs.

The National Library of Greece is one of the most important cultural institutions in the country and has a long history of serving the needs of researchers and students. It is an essential part of the cultural and intellectual life of the city of Athens and is a popular destination for visitors.

National Garden of Athens

The National Garden of Athens is located in the center of the city, near the Greek Parliament and the Tomb of the Unknown Soldier.

It is a beautiful and tranquil oasis of greenery, fountains, and sculptures, surrounded by some of the city's most famous landmarks.

The National Garden was originally established in 1836 by King Otto, the first King of Greece, to provide a space for relaxation and recreation. It covers an area of approximately 15 acres and contains over 500 species of plants, trees, and shrubs. The Garden is home to many species of birds, insects, and mammals, including the common sparrow, blackbird, and the rare Greek squirrel.

The National Garden contains a number of interesting features, such as the Zappeion building, a neoclassical structure built in the 19th century, and the Greek Prime Minister's Mansion, which is now used as a conference center. There are also a number of statues and sculptures scattered throughout the Garden, including the marble statue of Athena, the Goddess of Wisdom.

The National Garden of Athens is a popular destination for visitors and locals alike, and provides a pleasant and peaceful environment in which to relax and enjoy the beauty of the city. It is open to the public from sunrise to sunset every day and admission is free.

National Garden of Athens

Williams Gill

CHAPTER 6

Safety and Security Tips for travelling in Athens

Athens is generally a safe city with a low crime rate. Tourists should take the same precautions as they would in any large city when it comes to safety and security. Most tourist areas are well-lit and heavily patrolled by police, but be sure to stay within these areas at night if possible. When out and about, keep a close eye on your belongings. Report any suspicious individuals or activities to the police.

As with any destination, use common sense when it comes to safety in Athens.

General safety Tips for travelling in Athens

1. **Be aware of your surroundings** - When walking around Athens, it is important to stay alert and aware of your surroundings at all times. Be vigilant and never leave your belongings unattended.

If you feel unsafe, it is best to find a populated area or a place with lots of people.

2. **Know the areas to avoid** - There are certain areas of Athens that are known to have higher levels of criminal activity. It is best to research which areas to avoid before you visit.

3. **Don't carry large amounts of cash** - Carrying large amounts of cash while travelling in Athens is not recommended. Instead, use a credit/debit card or an ATM card as a form of payment.

4. **Invest in travel insurance** - It is important to invest in travel insurance when travelling to Athens. This way, you are covered for any medical emergencies or other unexpected costs that may arise during your trip.

5. **Stay in well-lit areas at night** - It is best to avoid dark alleys and secluded areas at night. It is advisable to stay in well-lit areas and to avoid travelling alone.

6. **Be aware of pickpockets** - Pickpocketing is common in Athens, so it is important to be aware of potential pickpockets in crowded areas. Keep your valuables close to your body and in secure pockets.

Health and Medical Care in Athens

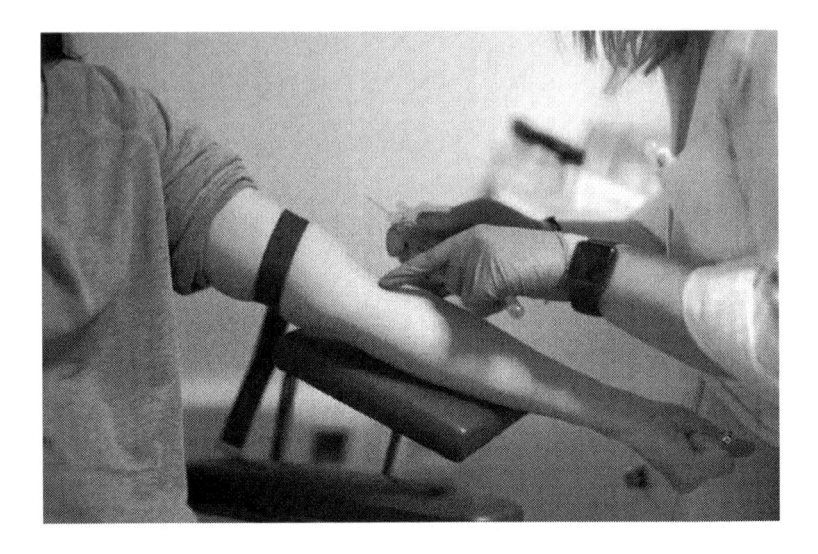

When it comes to health and medical care in Athens, visitors have plenty of options to choose from. Athens is renowned for its excellent medical care, with a wide range of hospitals, clinics and private health care providers.

When traveling to Athens, it is important to be aware of the country's healthcare system. The healthcare system in Greece is divided into two main categories – public and private.

The public healthcare system is funded by the government and is available to all citizens, regardless of their income. It is typically more affordable than the private sector, but it also tends to have longer wait times and less specialized services.

The private healthcare system in Athens is widely available, and is often favored by tourists due to its superior quality of care. There are numerous private hospitals, clinics and health care providers throughout Athens. Many of these are staffed by experienced physicians, nurses and other medical professionals, and are equipped with the latest medical technology. Private healthcare in Athens is usually more expensive than the public system, but it often provides quicker access to specialized services and more personalized care.

When it comes to emergency care, Athens has several well-equipped hospitals that provide 24-hour emergency services.

These hospitals are staffed by experienced medical personnel, and they are well-equipped to handle a variety of medical emergencies.

In addition to the hospitals, Athens also has numerous pharmacies, which can be found throughout the city. These pharmacies provide a wide range of over-the-counter medicines, as well as prescription medications. Pharmacies are also a great source of information about the healthcare system in Athens, and they can provide advice on where to find the best medical care.

In terms of preventive care, Athens has many public health centers and private clinics offering a range of services. These include vaccinations, screenings, and check-ups, as well as more specialized procedures.

Overall, Athens is an excellent destination for medical care. The city has a well-developed healthcare system that is supported by both public and private institutions. Visitors to Athens can rest assured that they will receive high-quality medical care, whether they choose to use the public system or the private sector.

Some hospitals in Athens include:

* **Evangelismo General Hospital** is the biggest public general hospital in Greece. It is located in Kolonaki, Athens.

* **Agios Andreas Hospital** located in Achaia, Greece.

* **Athens Medical Center** which is a private hospital in Maroussi, Athens.

* **The Daphni Psychiatric Hospital** is the largest hospital in Greece . It is located in Chaidari, Athens.

* **The Hygeia Hospital(Diagnostic and Therapeutic Center of Athens)** was the first private hospital in Greece.

* **Penteli Children's Hospital** which is located in Penteli, Athens.

* **Agios Panteleimonas Hospital** which is located in Nikaia, Athens.

* **Amalia Fleming Hospital** which is located in Melissa, Athens.

* **Alexandra General Hospital** which is located in Alexandroupoli.

Common Health Concerns in Athens

1. **Heat Stroke** – Heat stroke is a serious condition caused by prolonged exposure to high temperatures. It is important to stay hydrated and wear light, breathable clothing when traveling in Athens during the summer months.

2. **Air Pollution** – Athens has relatively high air pollution due to its population density and vehicle traffic. It is important to take precautions such as wearing a face mask and avoiding physical activity outdoors during peak pollution hours.

3. **Food Safety** – Food safety is an important concern when traveling in Athens. It is recommended to only eat at establishments with good hygiene ratings, and to avoid purchasing food from street vendors.

4. **Mosquito-Borne Illnesses** – Athens is located in a region where mosquito-borne illnesses such as malaria, dengue fever and West Nile Virus are present. It is important to take precautions to avoid mosquito bites, such as wearing long-sleeved clothing and using insect repellents.

5. **Sunburn** – Sunburn is a common health concern in Athens due to the hot summer sun. It is recommended to wear sunscreen with an SPF of 30 or higher, and to avoid spending long periods of time in direct sunlight.

Crimes to Watch Out for in Athens

1. **Pick pocketing:** Pick pocketing is a common problem in Athens, as in many tourist cities. Be aware of your surroundings, particularly in crowded public areas like markets, train stations, and busy streets. Avoid keeping valuables in your pockets and never leave your bags unattended.

2. **Street Fraud:** Fraudsters posing as police officers or tour guides will approach you on the street and ask to check your documents or wallet.

Always be suspicious of anyone who approaches you asking for money or documents.

3. **ATM Fraud:** ATM fraud is a common occurrence in Athens. Be careful to use ATMs that are located in secure locations and to cover your PIN when entering it into the machine.

4. **Fake or Counterfeit Goods:** Be wary of vendors who offer counterfeit goods. Be sure to check the quality of the product and ask for a receipt before making a purchase.

5. **Taxi Scams:** Unscrupulous taxi drivers will take advantage of unsuspecting tourists by overcharging them for their ride. Negotiate the fare before getting into the cab, and always ask for a receipt.

Williams Gill

Accommodation in Athens

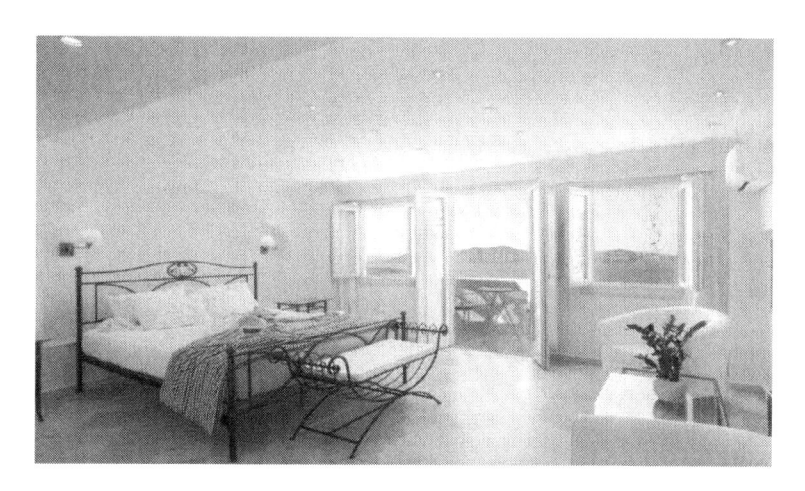

Athens has a wide variety of accommodation options to suit any budget. Whether you are looking for a luxury 5-star hotel, a budget hostel, or a self-catering apartment, you can find something to suit your needs in the Greek capital. Hotels in Athens can range from small family-run establishments to international chains, and there are plenty of hostels and apartments available for those on a tighter budget.

Airbnb(Air Bed and Breakfast) is also an increasingly popular choice for visitors to Athens, with many apartments available to short and long-term renters. There are also plenty of camping spots and caravan parks in the area, offering an affordable option for those who want to explore the region in a more natural setting.

Hotels and Resorts

1. **Hotel Grande Bretagne** – Located in Syntagma Square, the luxurious 5-star Hotel Grande Bretagne offers breathtaking views of the Acropolis and the Parliament. It features a rooftop restaurant, where guests can enjoy traditional Greek cuisine and international dishes.

2. **Electra Palace Hotel** – Situated in Plaka, the Electra Palace Hotel offers a variety of accommodation options, from luxury suites to family

rooms. The hotel's restaurant serves traditional Greek and Mediterranean dishes.

3. **AthensWas Hotel** – Located in Psirri, AthensWas Hotel is a modern, trendy hotel that offers boutique-style accommodation. Its restaurant serves Mediterranean cuisine with a twist.

4. **Hilton Athens** – Situated in the vibrant area of Kolonaki, the Hilton Athens is a luxurious 5-star hotel that offers excellent views of the Acropolis. Its restaurant serves international dishes and traditional Greek cuisine.

5. **Athens Gate Hotel** – Located in the Plaka district, the Athens Gate Hotel is a modern hotel with a great view of the Acropolis. It offers a variety of accommodation options and its restaurant serves traditional Greek and Mediterranean dishes.

6. **Divani Palace Acropolis** – Situated in the heart of Athens, the Divani Palace Acropolis is a luxurious 5-

star hotel that offers panoramic views of the Acropolis. Its restaurant serves traditional Greek cuisine and international dishes.

Camping

There are seven campsites in Athens and its vicinity, so the area contains more than a few. There are 6 campgrounds in Attica, and Greece offers a total of 178 campsites for you to enjoy while on vacation if you'd like to have more options.

Here, you may locate a campsite that best meets your requirements. The Milos Camping Pool is available to swimmers. A vacation without your dog is unthinkable, right? Your dog and you are welcome to camp in Athens. If you want to get a tan while staying at Camping Bacchus, go to the beach. Looking for a more hospitable strategy? At Camping Nea Makri, erect your tent.

Some major campsites include:

1. **Athens Camping:** Athens Camping is located in the heart of Athens, near the National Archaeological Museum. It offers a variety of camping options ranging from tents to cabins, as well as a restaurant and bar. It is close to many of Athens' popular attractions, including the Acropolis and the Plaka district.

2. **Athens Marina Camping:** Athens Marina Camping is located near the Marina of Athens and is ideal for those wishing to stay near the coast.

It offers a wide range of options for camping, including tents, cabins, and caravans. It also has a restaurant and bar, as well as a swimming pool and playground.

3. **Akadimia Camping:** Akadimia Camping is located near the University of Athens and offers a variety of camping options, including tents, cabins, and caravans. It also has a restaurant and bar, as well as a swimming pool and playground.

4. **Elliniko Camping:** Elliniko Camping is located near the Elliniko district of Athens and offers a variety of camping options, including tents, cabins, and caravans. It also has a restaurant and bar, as well as a swimming pool and playground.

5. **Vouliagmeni Camping:** Vouliagmeni Camping is located near the seaside town of Vouliagmeni and offers a variety of camping options, including tents, cabins, and caravans. It also has a restaurant and bar, as well as a swimming pool and playground.

6. **Glyfada Camping:** Glyfada Camping is located near the district of Glyfada and offers a variety of camping options, including tents, cabins, and caravans. It also has a restaurant and bar, as well as a swimming pool and playground.

7. **Athens Grand Hotel:** This luxury hotel is located in the affluent northern suburb of Kifissia. It offers a wide range of facilities, including a rooftop pool, a spa and a gym. Guests can also enjoy spacious rooms that are equipped with air conditioning, free Wi-Fi and private balconies with views of the Acropolis.

Parks and Resorts

With over 5,000 islands and a large mountainous mainland filled with natural wonders, Greece is a place for adventure lovers. When it comes to searching for places to stay in Athens, you might want to think a little out of place.

Let's take a look at some of the best places to settle down and have fun. Which one would you prefer?

1. **Athens Glamping:** Located just a few miles from downtown Athens, this unique camping site offers a unique blend of luxury and nature.

This campground has all the amenities of a luxury hotel and features gorgeous views of the Athens skyline. The campground has a variety of cabins, tents, and other lodging options, and each has a bathroom and kitchenette. Athens Glamping is a great location for those looking to camp in a comfortable, safe, and private setting.

2. **Athens Caravan Park:** This family-friendly campground is located near the Acropolis and offers a variety of camping and caravanning options. The campground has a range of facilities, including a playground, swimming pool, and a mini-market. The campground also has a bar and restaurant for visitors.

3. **Athens Camping Resort:** This camping resort is located in the heart of Athens and offers easy access to the city's attractions. The resort has a variety of different camping options, such as tents, cabins and RV sites. The resort also features a range of amenities, including a swimming pool, restaurants and bars, a playground, and more.

4. **Athens Beach Campground:** Located on the coast of Athens, this campground offers stunning views of the sea. The campground has a range of different camping options, including tent and RV sites, cabins, and beach houses. The campground also features a range of amenities, such as a swimming pool, restaurant, and bar.

5. **Athens National Park Campground:** This campground is located in the heart of Athens and offers a unique camping experience. The park has a variety of different camping options, including tent and RV sites, cabins, and beach houses.

The campground also has a range of amenities, including a swimming pool, restaurants and bars, a playground, and more.

6. **Athens Riverside Campground:** This riverside campground is located in the heart of Athens and offers stunning views of the nearby river. The campground has a variety of different camping

options, including tent and RV sites, cabins, and beach houses. The campground also features a range of amenities, such as a swimming pool, restaurant, and bar.

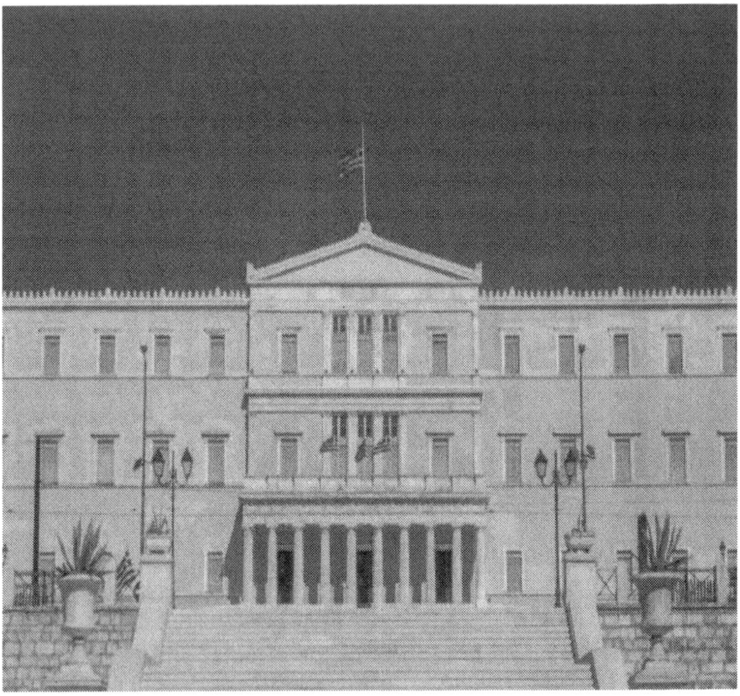

CHAPTER 8

Eating and Dining in Athens

Athens Cuisine: A Culinary Adventure

Athens is a city full of culture and history, but it is also a city that is known for its delicious cuisine. From traditional Greek dishes to flavors from all over the world, Athens has a restaurant for every taste.

For a truly authentic Greek experience, try some of the city's traditional dishes. Souvlaki, gyros, and moussaka are all staples of the cuisine. Souvlaki is a skewer of grilled meat, usually pork or chicken, served with pita bread or a salad. Gyros is a sandwich made of pork, chicken, or lamb that is cooked on a vertical rotisserie and served with tzatziki sauce. Moussaka is a classic Greek dish of layered eggplant and ground beef topped with béchamel sauce and baked in the oven.

For a more international experience, Athens has a wide variety of restaurants to choose from. Italian, Indian, Chinese, and American are all popular options, and can be found all around the city. Greek-style pizzas are also a popular choice, topped with feta cheese, olives, and other traditional ingredients.

If you're looking for something lighter and more traditional, try some of the city's famous street food. Loukoumades are deep-fried dough balls that are served with honey and cinnamon, and bougatsa is a pastry filled with custard or cheese.

Koulouri is a circular bread ring sprinkled with sesame seeds, and loukaniko is a type of sausage.

For a sweet treat, try some of Greece's famous desserts. Baklava is a rich, sweet pastry made of layers of filo pastry filled with nuts and honey. Galaktoboureko is a custard-filled pastry made with a light syrup, and kataifi is a shredded pastry filled with nuts, honey, and cinnamon.

Athens is also home to a variety of seafood restaurants, where you can try some of the freshest seafood in the country. Favourites include grilled fish, fried calamari, and Greek-style seafood stews.

Some of these foods in Details:

1. **Souvlaki:** Souvlaki is a popular Greek dish of grilled meat (usually pork, chicken, or lamb) served on skewers with grilled bread or pita. It can be found at many traditional restaurants and street vendors throughout Athens.

2. **Gyros:** Gyros is a type of sandwich made with grilled, seasoned meat (usually pork or chicken) served on pita bread with lettuce, tomato, onion, and tzatziki sauce. It is a popular street food in Athens and is also served at many restaurants throughout the city.

3. **Moussaka:** Moussaka is a traditional Greek dish of eggplant, potatoes, and minced meat baked with a creamy béchamel sauce and topped with cheese. It is a popular dish in Greece and can be found at many restaurants throughout Athens.

4. **Greek Salad:** Greek Salad is a traditional dish of chopped tomatoes, cucumbers, onions, olives, feta cheese, and oregano dressed with olive oil and lemon juice. It is a popular side dish in Athens and is served as an appetizer at many restaurants throughout the city.

5. **Tiropita:** Tiropita is a traditional Greek cheese pie made with layers of phyllo dough and a filling of feta cheese, eggs, and butter.

It is a popular snack in Athens and can be found at many bakeries and restaurants throughout the city.

6. **Loukoumades:** Loukoumades are small honey-drenched Greek donuts served with a variety of toppings such as cinnamon, nuts, and honey. They are a popular sweet treat in Athens and can be found at many bakeries and street vendors throughout the city.

7. **Pastitsio:** Pastitsio is a traditional Greek dish of macaroni, ground beef, tomatoes, and béchamel sauce baked in layers and topped with cheese.

It is a popular dish in Athens and can be found at many restaurants throughout the city.

8. **Greek Coffee:** Greek Coffee is a traditional Greek beverage made with finely ground coffee beans and sugar. It is a popular drink in Athens and can be found at many cafes and restaurants throughout the city.

No matter what type of cuisine you're looking for, you're sure to find something delicious in Athens.

With its wide selection of restaurants, there's something for everyone in this vibrant city.

Regional Athens Food to Try

Athens regional cuisine is an intriguing and delicious mix of flavours, both old and new. The city is known for its traditional dishes, such as Souvlaki, Gyro and Moussaka, as well as its more modern interpretations of classic ingredients. The city is also renowned for its fresh seafood, with a variety of fish and shellfish dishes available.

Greek staples such as olives, feta cheese, and olive oil are also ubiquitous in Athens, with many dishes featuring these ingredients. Athenians also enjoy street food such as Koulouri, a type of circular bread, and Kebab, a grilled meat sandwich. With so many options for food lovers, Athens is a great place to explore the culinary delights of Greece.

1. **Dolmades:** Dolmades are grape leaves filled with a mixture of rice, herbs, and spices. They are often served as an appetizer or side dish in traditional Greek restaurants in Athens.

2. **Baklava:** Baklava is a traditional Greek pastry made with layers of phyllo dough, honey, and nuts. It is often served as a dessert in traditional Greek restaurants in Athens.

Athens Wine

Athens is home to a rich and vibrant wine culture. Wines from the region have been highly regarded for centuries and are now some of the most sought-after wines in the world. The region boasts a wide variety of grape varietals, styles, and quality levels. The most popular varietals are Savatiano, Assyrtiko, Moschofilero, and Agiorgitiko. These grapes are often blended together to create unique and flavorful blends.

The vast majority of wines made in Athens are white and range from dry, crisp whites to sweet dessert wines. Red wines are also produced, typically from Agiorgitiko grapes, and are usually full-bodied and well-balanced. Whether you're looking for a special occasion bottle or just a casual glass of wine, Athens has something for everyone.

Athens wine is a regional specialty of the Greek capital. There are five main types of wine produced in the area: Nemea, Mantinia, Attica, Peloponnese, and Retsina.

Nemea is a red wine made from the Agiorgitiko grape and considered one of the best wines in the country. It has a bright ruby color and a spicy, fruity flavor. It is usually dry and pairs well with lamb, beef, and game dishes.

Mantinia is a white wine made from the Moschofilero grape, usually with a light body and a crisp, fruity flavor. It is typically dry, with a slight hint of sweetness, and is great with fish, salads, and light dishes.

Attica is an interesting red blend made from a variety of native grape varieties, including Agiorgitiko and Mavro. It has a deep ruby color and a full body flavor, with notes of blackberry and spice. It pairs well with strong, hearty dishes and barbecued meats.

Peloponnese is a white wine made from the Savatiano grape. It has a light body and a pleasant, sweet-tart flavor, with a slight hint of honey. It pairs well with fish, pasta dishes, and salads.

Finally, **Retsina** is a white wine that is made with resin. It has a distinctive flavor, with notes of pine and lemon, and is typically dry and acidic. It pairs well with Greek-style dishes, such as moussaka and souvlaki.

Athens wines can be found in most Greek supermarkets and wine shops, as well as in some tourist shops. They are also available in many restaurants and bars in the city.

Best Places to Eat in Athens

1. **O Thanasis:** Located in the Monastiraki district of Athens, O Thanasis is a beloved spot for traditional Greek gyros. The restaurant has been around since the 1960s and is known for its friendly staff and delicious food. The menu includes classic gyros, souvlaki, and various other Greek dishes.

2. **Funky Gourmet:** Considered one of the best restaurants in Athens, Funky Gourmet is a Michelin-starred restaurant serving up creative twists on traditional Greek dishes. Located in the Kolonaki

district, Funky Gourmet offers a multi-course tasting menu that changes seasonally.

3. **Stani:** Located in the trendy Psyrri district, Stani is an upscale taverna serving up traditional Greek cuisine. The menu includes Greek classics such as moussaka, pastitsio, and souvlaki. The restaurant also boasts a great selection of Greek wines and beers.

4. **Avli:** Located in the chic area of Kolonaki, Avli is a modern Greek taverna that serves up delicious cuisine in an elegant atmosphere. The menu offers a wide selection of traditional Greek dishes, including grilled seafood, house-made pasta, and marinated meats.

5. **Kostarelos:** Located in the Plaka neighborhood, Kostarelos is a popular spot for traditional Greek sweets.

The shop has been around since 1920 and is known for its fresh, handmade desserts. Kostarelos specializes in loukoumades (honey-soaked doughnuts) and other Greek specialties.

6. **Kriti:** Located in the Psirri neighborhood, Kriti is a modern Greek restaurant that serves up delicious seafood dishes. The menu includes a wide selection of fresh fish and seafood, as well as classic Greek dishes such as moussaka and tzatziki.

Williams Gill

Williams Gill

Part III

Travel Essentials

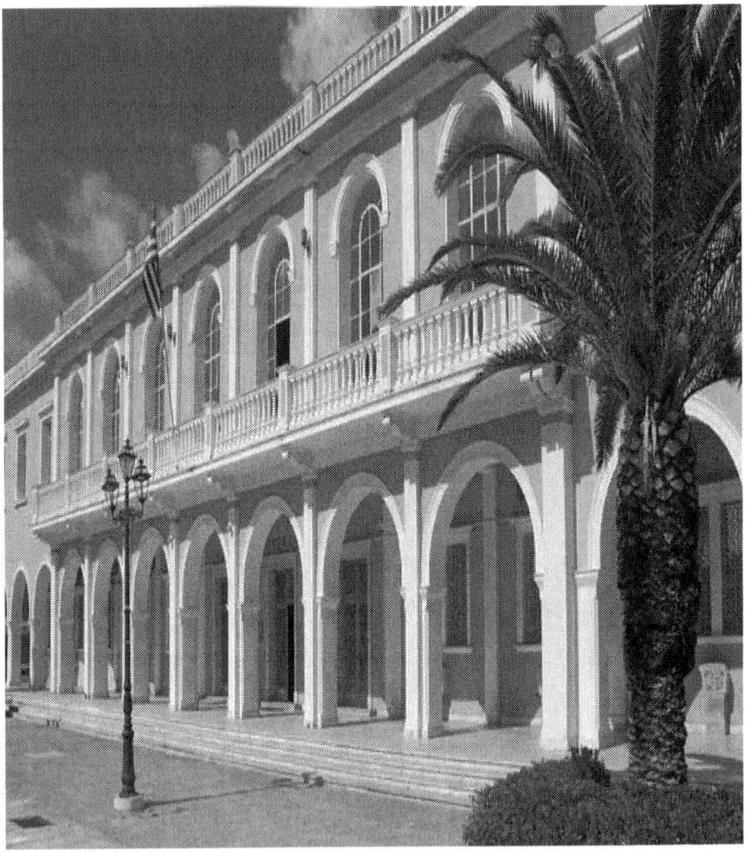

CHAPTER 9

Financial Matters

Currency and Exchange Rates in Athens

The currency of Greece is the Euro (€). Current exchange rates for the Euro vary, but as of 2023(Time of writing this book), 1 Euro is equal to approximately 1.091 US Dollars. When traveling to Athens, it is important to be aware of the current exchange rate to ensure you are receiving the most accurate value for your money.

Exchange rates may vary depending on where you exchange money, so it is best to shop around and compare rates. Credit cards are widely accepted in Athens, so it is important to check with your card issuer regarding any fees associated with using the card abroad.

Credit Card and ATMs in Athens

Credit cards and ATMs are widely accepted in Athens and Greece as a whole, with most major banks and establishments accepting MasterCard, Visa, American Express, and Maestro. Visitors are advised to bring a valid passport and inform their credit card company before travelling to Greece, as credit card companies may block transactions due to security measures.

ATMs are available in Greece, with most major banks having them readily available. Most ATMs will accept foreign cards, however, visitors should be aware that some may not.

Under Greek Government law, visitors are allowed to use their foreign credit cards, provided they are able to prove their legal identity and the validity of the card. Visitors should also be aware that there may be additional fees associated with using their foreign credit cards, so it is advisable to check with their bank before travelling.

Additionally, visitors should keep their credit card, ATM card, and other financial documents safe and secure.

Williams Gill

CHAPTER 10

Traveling With Kids or Pets

Traveling to Athens with kids can be an exciting and rewarding experience. It is Greece's capital city, and the birthplace of democracy, western philosophy, and the Olympic Games. Athens is filled with ancient monuments, stunning views, and fascinating history. While there are definitely some great things to do with kids in Athens, there are also some potential pitfalls that parents need to be aware of before they plan their trip.

One of the major pros of traveling to Athens with kids is that there are a number of great attractions and experiences that they can enjoy. From the Acropolis and Parthenon to the National Archaeological Museum, kids will find plenty of interesting things to explore and learn about. The city also has a vibrant nightlife and plenty of great restaurants, making it a great place for family dining.

On the other hand, there are some potential downsides to traveling to Athens with kids. For one thing, it can be a bit overwhelming for younger children. The city is incredibly crowded and busy, and the streets can be chaotic and noisy.

Additionally, Athens can be quite hot in the summer months, making it uncomfortable for kids. Finally, there are some safety concerns that parents should be aware of. Pickpocketing is an issue in Athens, so it's important to be vigilant and keep an eye on your belongings.

Overall, traveling to Athens with kids can be a great experience, but it's important to be aware of the potential pitfalls. Make sure to plan ahead and research the best places to go and the safety concerns that you should watch out for. With a bit of preparation and planning, you can have an amazing trip to Athens with your kids.

Pets

Traveling with pets on vacation to Athens can be an exciting and rewarding experience, but it is important to plan ahead and do your research to ensure a safe and enjoyable experience for both you and your pet.

The laws in Athens vary, but it is generally accepted that pets must be kept on a leash and must not be allowed to wander in public areas. Additionally, pet owners are expected to clean up after their pet and make sure their pet is not disturbing other people or animals.

Fortunately, pet-friendly accommodations are easy to find in Athens, with many hotels and Airbnb listings offering pet-friendly options. However, it is important to make sure that the accommodation you choose is properly equipped to keep your pet safe and comfortable. Additionally, some accommodations may have additional policies concerning pets, so make sure to read the fine print and contact the accommodation before booking to make sure your pet is welcome.

When it comes to transportation, there are some options available. Public transportation may be an option for smaller pets, but keep in mind that larger pets may not be allowed on public transportation. Additionally, pet-friendly taxis and private car services are available in Athens, but it is important to make sure that the company is aware that your pet is traveling with you and that you are aware of any additional fees or charges that may apply.

Overall, traveling with pets to Athens can be a great experience, as long as you are aware of the local laws and regulations and make sure to properly plan and prepare for the trip. With the right planning and preparation, you and your pet can have a safe and enjoyable trip to Athens.

CHAPTER 11

Communication

Communicating as a visitor to Athens can be an enjoyable and rewarding experience. Although English is widely spoken in the city, the official language of Greece is Greek, so it is important to learn a few phrases in order to communicate effectively with the locals.

In Athens, the most commonly spoken language is Greek. Knowing a few basic words and phrases will go a long way in helping you to have successful interactions with the people you meet in Athens. If you are able to read and write Greek, even better.

In addition to learning Greek, it is also important to be mindful of the local customs and etiquette in order to ensure a positive exchange. It is important to be respectful of the local culture, including the local dress code, which is generally conservative.

Avoid public displays of affection and speak in a polite and courteous manner. It is also important to be aware of the local non-verbal communication and body language, which can be quite different from what is expected in other countries.

When communicating with locals in Athens, it is important to be patient and polite. Most people in Athens are friendly and welcoming and will be happy to help you if you need assistance. However, it is important to be aware that some locals may not speak English and may not be very open to discussing their culture or politics. If this is the case, it is best to move on to another topic of discussion.

Here are some tips for effectively communicating with the people of Athens:

1. Learn some basic Greek words and phrases.

2. Be mindful of local customs and etiquette.

3. Speak in a polite and courteous manner.

4. Respect non-verbal communication and body language.

5. Be patient and polite.

6. Do not discuss politics or religion.

7. Move on to another topic if the conversation becomes uncomfortable.

By following these tips, you will be able to communicate effectively with the people of Athens, and have a positive experience in the city.

Important Greek Words and Phrases

Learning to say a few greetings is an important gesture when travelling anywhere around the globe and the Greeks do appreciate the little attempt, however good or bad it is. It's something to be proud of as a visitor.

During my stay there, I learnt a few words which I am going to share with you in this guide.

Basic Greek Words and Pronunciation

ENGLISH	GREEK	SOUND
Good Morning	Καλημέρα	ka-li-me-ra
Good Night	Καληνύχτα	ka-li-ni-hta
Good Evening	Καλησπέρα	ka-li-spe-ra
Hello/Goodbye	Γειά Σας	yia-sas
Yes	Ναι	ne
No	Όχι	o-hi
Sorry/Excuse me	Συγνώμη	sig-no-mii

More Greek words

Παρακαλώ (Pa-ra-ka-lo) – Please or You're welcome

Πού είναι (Poo ee-ne) - Where is?

Πως είναι (Pohs ee-ne) - How is?

Μιλάτε αγγλικά (mi-la-te a-gli-ka)- Do you speak English?

Δεν καταλαβαίνω (then-ka-ta-la-ve-noh)- I don't understand

Χαίρω Πολύ (heh-ro po-li)- Nice to meet you

Μου αρέσει η Ελλάδα (mou a-resi i E-la-tha)- I like Greece

Παρακαλώ με (Pa-ra-ka-lo me) - Please help me

Ευχαριστώ πολύ (Ef-ha-ree-sto po-lee) - Thank you very much

Πού μπορώ να βρω (Poo bor-oh na vroh) - Where can I find?

Πως μπορώ να φτάσω (Pohs bor-oh na ftah-so) - How can I get there?

Ποια είναι η διαδρομή (Pia ee-ne ee dia-dro-mee) - What is the route?

Πόσο κοστίζει (Pos-oh kos-tee-zee) - How much does it cost?

Τι κάνεις (Tee kanis?)- How are you?

Καλά, ευχαριστώ (Kala, efharisto)- I'm fine, thank you

Πώς σε λένε (Pos se leneh?)- What is your name?

Με λένε... (Me leneh...)- My name is...

Τι ώρα είναι (Ti hora ineh?)- What time is it?

Γεια μας! (Yamas!)- Cheers! (when drinking)

Ώπα! (Opahh!)- Όπα! (when dancing)

Immersing yourself in the local language of the Greek is the best way to enjoy your stay in Athens!

CONCLUSION

As we come to the end of this insightful journey into the vibrant city of Athens, All tourists and visitors should know that Athens is an amazing city that offers a plethora of exciting cultural experiences and a host of incredible attractions. From its iconic landmarks to its diverse cuisine, Athens is a magical destination that will captivate your senses and leave you in awe.

To truly get the most out of this city, I recommend that you plan your trip well in advance and familiarize yourself with all the necessary travel tips before your arrival. This will ensure that you make the most of your time in Athens and avoid any potential pitfalls.

Additionally, it is important to explore all the amazing attractions and sights that this city has to offer. From visiting the Acropolis and the Parthenon to exploring the cobbled streets of Plaka or the historic neighborhoods of Monastiraki, Athens has something for everyone.

The topics in this book have been written to help you make the most of your visit to the beautiful city of Athens and I trust that you will be able to experience all this city has to offer.

In conclusion, the Athens Travel Guide has been invaluable in helping readers explore the city and experience the best it has to offer. This comprehensive guidebook provides detailed information on the city's many attractions, from historical sites to cultural experiences, and provides tips on how to get around and make the most of your stay.

It also offers insight into the city's gastronomy and nightlife, as well as advice on where to find the best deals. With its detailed information, easy-to-follow maps, and helpful tips and advice, readers are sure to get the most out of their Athens experience.

Finally, I hope that this book has provided you with all the essential information you need to make your trip to Athens a remarkable experience.

Whether you're a first-time visitor or a seasoned traveler, the Athens Travel Guide is an invaluable resource in helping you make the most of your time in Athens. Enjoy the sights, savor the flavors, and create memories that will last a lifetime. Safe travels!

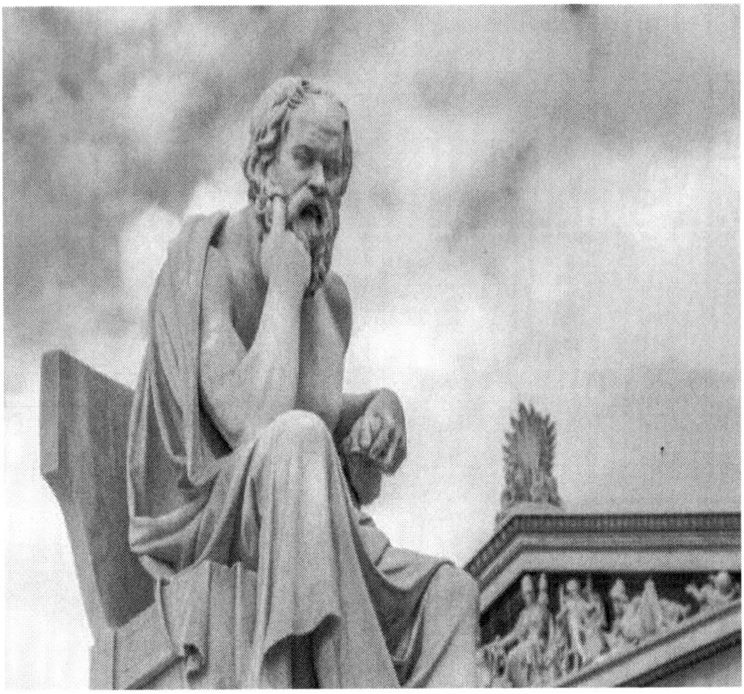

Street Map of Athens   Courtesy:MapBox

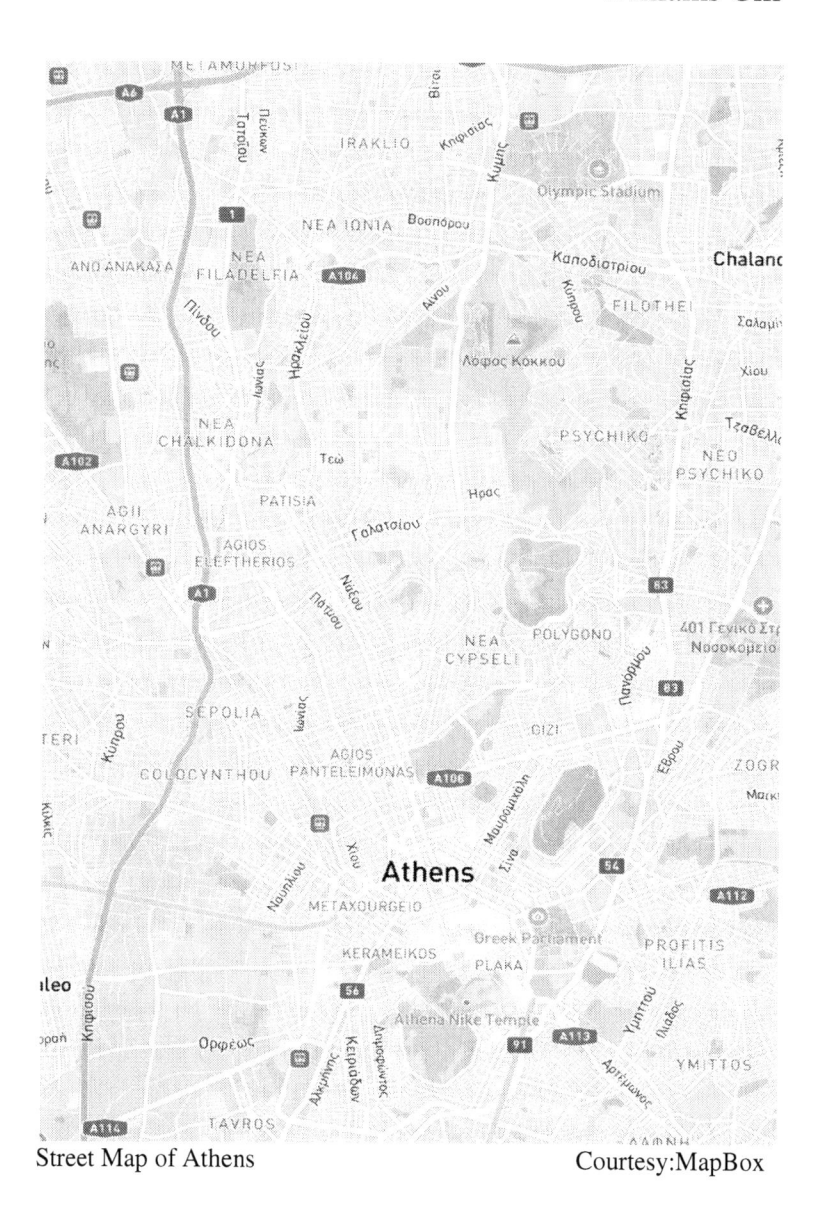

Williams Gill

Notes

Notes

Printed in Great Britain
by Amazon